D1436766

SPACE SCIENCE

SCIENCE FOR SURVIVING IN SPACE

Mark Thompson

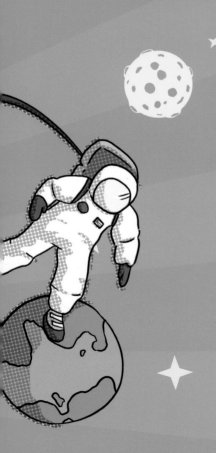

WAYLAND
www.waylandbooks.co.uk

First published in Great Britain in 2019
by Wayland
Copyright © Hodder and Stoughton, 2019
All rights reserved

Editor: Amy Pimperton
Design and illustration: Collaborate

ISBN: 978 1 5263 0843 6

Printed and bound in China

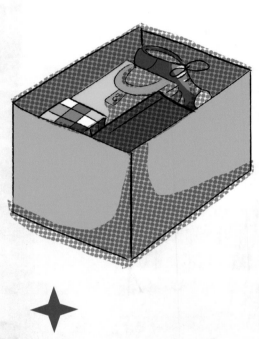

Wayland, an imprint of
Hachette Children's Group
Part of Hodder and Stoughton
Carmelite House
50 Victoria Embankment
London EC4Y 0DZ

An Hachette UK Company

www.hachette.co.uk
www.hachettechildrens.co.uk

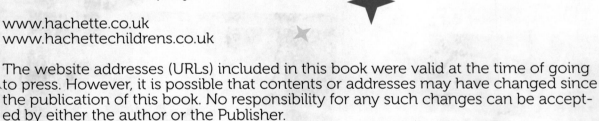

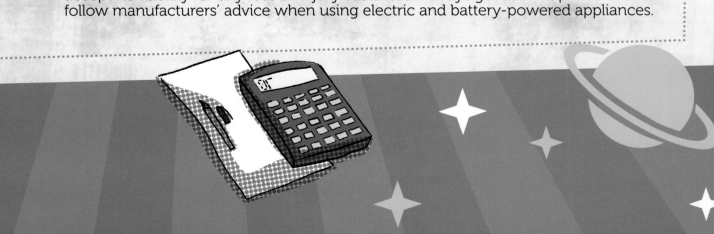

CONTENTS

A DANGEROUS PLACE

If you could get into space without a rocket or spacesuit for protection then you might be surprised to learn that you would be able to survive ... but only for a very short time. Starved of much-needed oxygen, after about fifteen seconds you would be unconscious. A few minutes later you would be dead. That's not something you'd want to try!

UNDER PRESSURE

A word of warning: DO NOT hold your breath if you suddenly find yourself in space. Your lungs are full of gas at normal pressure, but the vacuum of space is low pressure. If you hold your breath the difference in pressure will make your lungs will blow up!

PERSONAL SPACE

In 1961 Yuri Gagarin (1934–68) was the first person in space and since then we have learned a lot about how to survive there. If you want to be an astronaut and travel in space then there is a lot to think about, but one of the main things is that we need air to breathe.

A spacecraft can provide that and give us warm rooms to live in, but to go out into space you need a spacesuit, which is just like your own personal spacecraft. Spacesuits have an air supply, keep your body at a constant temperature and even have an inbuilt toilet!

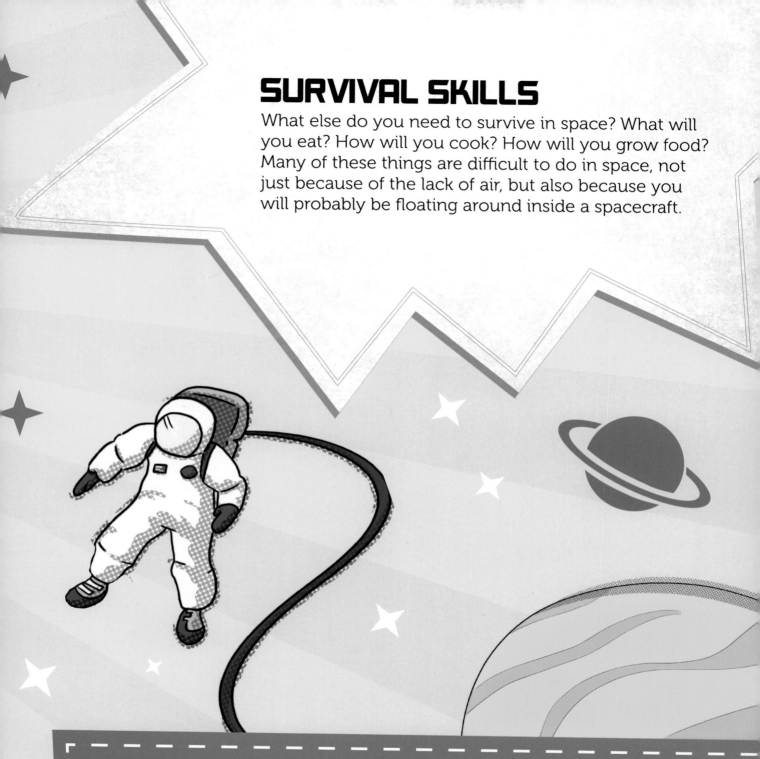

SURVIVAL SKILLS

What else do you need to survive in space? What will you eat? How will you cook? How will you grow food? Many of these things are difficult to do in space, not just because of the lack of air, but also because you will probably be floating around inside a spacecraft.

EXPLORE

There are dangers in space too, such as rocks flying around that could hit you and radiation from the Sun, which can make you very ill. In this book, we look at twelve activities to help you explore what it might be like to live – and survive – in space.

PACK A SPACE BAG

Journeys into space can last for months and there is no washing machine for your clothes or shop to buy things. Astronauts must take everything they need for the whole journey. Most things are packed for them, but they are allowed to take some personal items, such as photographs.

There is very little room, so they can only take a few items. If you were going on a space voyage what would you take with you? In this activity you will work out whether you can fit in everything you want to take.

YOU WILL NEED:

- a small box
- a ruler
- a calculator
- a pen
- a piece of paper
- weighing scales
- some personal objects

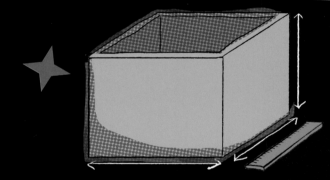

1 To find the volume of your box, measure its height, width and depth in cm and then multiply them all together.

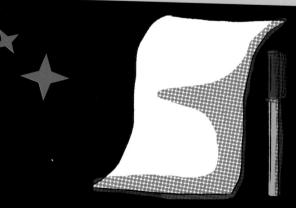

2 Make a list of things that you would like to take with you.

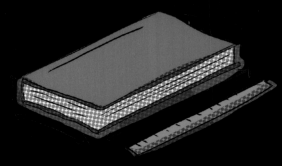

3 Measure the height, width and depth of each item on your list in cm and note them down.

4 Next, work out the volume of each item. Write down the answers and then add all the answers together.

If this number is a smaller number than the volume of the box then everything should fit. If it is a larger number then you have too many things and will have to take something out.

5 Weigh each item on the scales and then add their weights together. This is important because you have a weight limit of 1.5 kg.

If the total weight is over 1,500 g then swap some of the heavier items for something lighter. You will also have to work out the volume of any new objects to see if they will fit in your box.

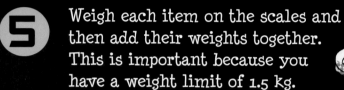

6 Once you have worked out that everything fits, pack them into your box to check if you are right.

SPACE FACT

Astronauts going to the International Space Station (ISS) can take just 1 kg of personal items. Next time you go to the shops, pick up a 1 kg bag of sugar to give you an idea of how little that is.

INFLATE A BALLOON ... WITH MICROBES

Life on Earth comes in lots of shapes and sizes. The smallest are known as microorganisms, or microbes. Many microbes, such as bacteria, can survive in very hostile conditions, such as extreme heat or cold. It might be that the first signs of life we find on another planet are microbes.

Scientists study microbes in space because they are small, easy to transport and don't feel pain like other more complex living things, such as dogs. You can study microbes in your kitchen at home. Bakers' yeast is a microscopic fungus used to make bread. In this activity we will see that yeast is a living thing as it helps us to blow up a balloon!

YOU WILL NEED:

- a clear, clean and empty plastic drinks bottle
- some warm water
- a packet of yeast
- a teaspoon
- some sugar
- a balloon

2

When yeast is cold and dry it cannot grow. Add it to the warm water to activate it and give the bottle a swirl to mix it in.

1

Fill the drinks bottle with about 4 cm of warm water.

3 Like many living things, yeast needs oxygen and food to grow. There is already air in the bottle, so add a teaspoon of sugar to the water and yeast mixture.

4 Place the balloon over the neck of the bottle and leave it in a warm place for about 30 minutes.

5 Check your balloon regularly and you should find that it has been blown up by the yeast!

As the yeast microbes use up the oxygen and eat the sugar, they give off a gas called carbon dioxide (the same gas that we breathe out), which blows up the balloon.

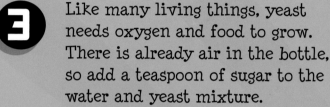

SPACE FACT

A tardigrade is a micro-animal that is about 0.5 mm long! These tiny animals are pretty tough and can survive in space for up to 10 days with no spacesuit or spacecraft to protect them.

EAT LIKE AN ASTRONAUT

On Earth, the force of gravity causes the liquids in your body, such as blood, to fall towards your feet. Your heart works against gravity by pumping the blood back up. In space, astronauts experience weightlessness, which makes the liquids spread around the body. This is called fluid shift. One side effect is that it blocks up the nose – a bit like when you have a cold.

Being able to smell is a really important part of being able to taste food. In space, fluid shift means astronauts cannot taste food very well, so they often prefer very strong flavours. This activity shows you how hard it is to taste food in space.

YOU WILL NEED:

- a peach
- a pear
- an apple
- a potato
- a knife
- a chopping board
- a blindfold
- a friend
- a glass of water
- a pen and a piece of paper

1 Ask an adult to help you prepare the food. Cut two slices of each food item and then put on your blindfold.

2 Ask your friend to line up the food so that there are two slices of each food together.

RED ALERT!
Ask an adult to help you use the knife.

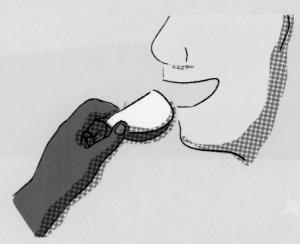

3 Pinch your nose and ask your friend to pass you one of each of the slices, one at a time. Take a bite and try to guess what each food is. Take a sip of water between each item. Ask your friend to write down your answers.

4 Our sense of taste relies on air moving around between the mouth and nose. Pinching your nose mimics the fluid shift effect as it stops the flow of air, making it much harder to taste. Un-pinch your nose and try again, testing the remaining food slices in the same order as in step 3.

5 Take the blindfold off and look at how you did on the first attempt. How much easier was it to taste the food the second time?

SPACE FACT
Astronauts on the ISS always try to get really spicy, tasty food because their sense of taste is affected by fluid shift. They often add hot pepper sauce to any meal they can to give it a stronger flavour.

WARM UP
WITH
INSULATION

Astronauts are kept warm in a heated spacecraft. But keeping your body at a constant temperature outside a spacecraft is a little bit harder, because temperatures in space can vary a lot.

When you lie in bed your duvet traps the heat from your body to keep you nice and warm. This trapping of heat is called insulation. Remove the insulation (the duvet) and you will get cold. Some materials are better at insulating than others. In this experiment we look at different materials to see how well they insulate against the cold.

YOU WILL NEED:

- three large and three smaller recyclable cups (like the ones you get from coffee shops)
- aluminium foil
- cotton wool
- paper
- some cold water

 1 Place one small recyclable cup inside each of the larger ones.

 **2** Scrunch up the aluminium foil and place it inside one of the larger cups so that it completely surrounds the smaller cup.

3 Rip the cotton wool into pieces and surround the second smaller cup with it. Scrunch up the paper and surround the third cup with it.

4 Carefully pour the same amount of cold water into each of the smaller cups. Take care not to drip any water on the insulation materials. Carefully put everything inside a freezer. Make sure the cups are level and upright!

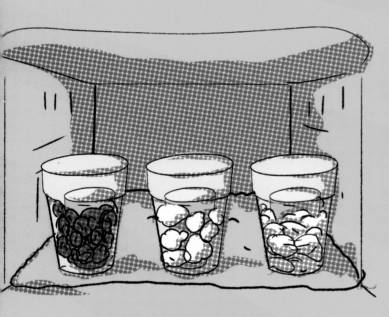

5 Check inside the freezer at regular intervals to see which cup of water freezes first. The water surrounded by the best insulator will take longest to freeze. Which one is it?

SPACE FACT

Temperatures in space can be very high and very low. If you floated around Earth, then on the daytime side you would be able to record temperatures as high as 260 °C, but on the night side, the temperature can get as low as -100 °C.

SHIELD YOURSELF FROM METEOROIDS

A meteoroid is a piece of rock or metal travelling through space. Over 500,000 meteoroids hurtling around Earth are larger than a marble, and there are millions of micrometeoroids and pieces of space dust that are smaller than a pin head. All of them travel at up to 28,100 km per hour (km/h) – that's much faster than a bullet!

Even a micrometeoroid can do a lot of damage. Spacesuits are made from many layers of materials to protect astronauts from these flying objects ripping their spacesuits. In this experiment we replicate a spacesuit's layers with newspaper and find out how many layers it will take to stop an marble from breaking through them.

YOU WILL NEED:

- some sheets of newspaper (preferably from a newspaper that has not been stapled together)
- a large marble or other small, heavy object you have asked permission to use
- lots of heavy books
- two dining chairs
- a cushion

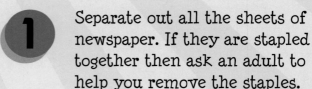

1 Separate out all the sheets of newspaper. If they are stapled together then ask an adult to help you remove the staples.

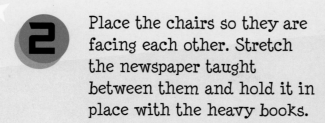

2 Place the chairs so they are facing each other. Stretch the newspaper taught between them and hold it in place with the heavy books.

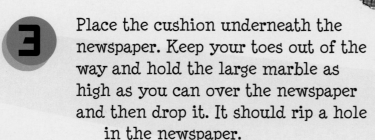

3 Place the cushion underneath the newspaper. Keep your toes out of the way and hold the large marble as high as you can over the newspaper and then drop it. It should rip a hole in the newspaper.

4 Repeat the experiment, replacing the ripped sheets and adding in an extra sheet each time, until you have enough sheets of paper to stop the marble from ripping through them. How many layers do you have?

INVESTIGATE

Try to find out how many layers a real spacesuit is made from. Do you think newspaper would be a suitable material to use in space?

GROW FOOD IN SPACE

Plants need food, air, light and warmth to grow. Conditions on Earth are perfect for the plants that grow here. You could take plant seeds into space, but providing air, warmth and light would not be easy, especially on an alien planet.

If you were to jump in a spacecraft and travel to Neptune's moon, Triton, then you would definitely have to provide your own light and warmth for plants to grow. This great activity shows how important these two things are by growing two lots of cress seeds, one with plenty of warmth and light, the other with neither.

YOU WILL NEED:

- some water
- two small plates
- two paper towels
- a teaspoon
- a packet of cress seeds
- one large cup or small bowl that will fit over the paper towel
- a fridge

1 Fold a paper towel into a small square. Repeat with the second paper towel and plate.

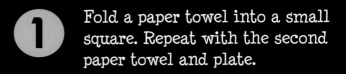

3 Sprinkle a teaspoon of cress seeds on to each paper towel. Try to get roughly the same amount of seeds on each paper towel.

2 Slowly drip water on to the paper towels until they are wet.

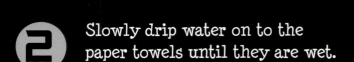

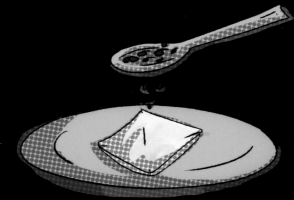

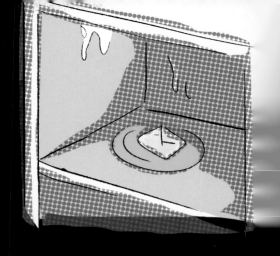

4 Place one plate of seeds on a windowsill where it will get light and warmth.

5 Place the bowl or cup over the other cress seeds and place them in a fridge so that they don't get any light or warmth. (This is a bit like wh it might be like for them on Neptune's moon, Triton.)

6 Look at the seeds every day and make sure that the paper towels are wet. Water them a little if they are dry. It may take a few days before you see any growth, but you should see that the plants getting warmth and light are growing well. The seeds in the cold and dark will probably not grow at all.

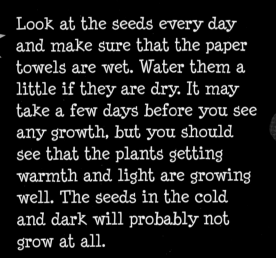

SCIENCE FACT

Neptune is the furthest planet from the Sun in the Solar System. At 4.5 billion km away from the Sun it is 30 times further away than Earth is from the Sun. At that distance, heat and light have so far to travel that the Sun would appear as a very bright star. Midday would be as bright as late evening and the temperature would be a chilly -214 °C.

DRAW A MAGNETIC FORCE FIELD

The Sun emits waves of energy, called radiation, that include light waves, heat waves and microwaves. Some radiation waves can harm living things.

Earth is a bit like a giant magnet. It has two magnetic poles that are attracted to each other. This pull between the magnetic North Pole and the magnetic South Pole creates invisible magnetic field lines, which create a magnetic field that protects us from the Sun's radiation. It's a bit like a force field that surrounds Earth.

In space we are not protected by Earth's force field, so scientists experiment with magnets to find ways to protect astronauts from radiation. In this experiment you will find the invisible magnetic field lines of a magnet.

YOU WILL NEED:

- a magnet (ideally a bar magnet)
- a navigational compass
- a pencil
- a piece of paper

1 Place the magnet in the centre of the piece of paper.

2 Put the compass at one end of the magnet and put a dot on the paper to show where the compass's arrow head is pointing.

3 Move the compass so that the end of its arrow is on top of the dot. Make another dot where the compass's arrow head is pointing.

4 Keep doing this until you get to the other end of the magnet.

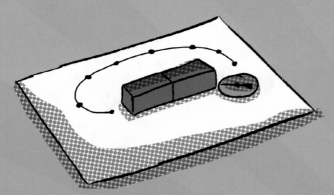

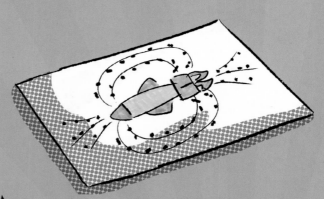

5 Join up the dots to show a magnetic field line. Start again at a different point on the magnet to create another magnetic field line. Repeat until the magnet is surrounded by magnetic field lines.

6 Draw a spacecraft where the magnet was to see the force field that could protect it from radiation in space.

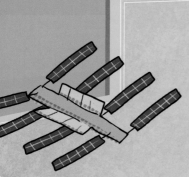

SPACE FACT

Exposure to radiation is measured in sieverts (Sv). The ISS orbits Earth at a distance where it is still protected from radiation by Earth's magnetic field. Even so, astronauts on the ISS experience 0.5 Sv, which is ten times more than we experience on the surface of Earth. Any more than that and the astronauts may become ill.

MAKE A BIOSPHERE ... IN A JAR!

In the future, humans may live on other planets where it might not be warm enough to grow food. The temperature on the surface of Mars, for example, is on average -55 °Celsius – too cold to grow food.

We would need to find a way to increase the temperature. One way is to make a biosphere, which is a building that mimics the conditions of Earth's ecosystems. It is like a greenhouse, which concentrates the Sun's rays through glass windows to raise the temperature on the inside. You can test how this works by making a tiny biosphere of your own.

YOU WILL NEED:

- two clean, empty jam jars
- some water
- six ice cubes
- two thermometers (optional)
- a small see-through plastic bag, large enough to cover the opening of one of the jars
- an elastic band

2 Add three ice cubes to each jar. If you want to use thermometers then add one to each jar.

Place the plastic bag over one of the jars. Seal it by placing the elastic band tightly around the neck of the jar.

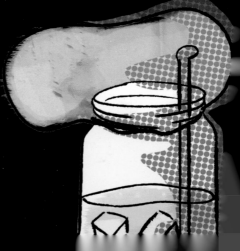

1

Half fill both jars with cold water.

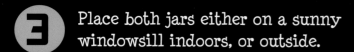

3 Place both jars either on a sunny windowsill indoors, or outside.

4 If you are using thermometers, take a look at both of them every half hour for two hours. Record the temperatures. If not, simply watch the ice cubes and see which ones melt the quickest.

5 You should find that the jar with the plastic bag warms up more quickly. This is because the Sun's energy can get in through the bag, but the heat cannot get out again.

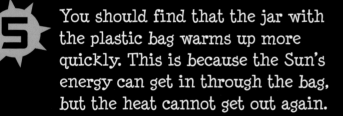

SCIENCE FACT

Biosphere 2 in Arizona, USA, has been used to test what it would be like to live on another planet. In 1994, eight people lived inside it for two years, completely shut off from the outside world.

MAKE DIRTY WATER CLEAN (ISH!)

Astronauts have lived in the ISS continuously since 2000, and most of the water they use on-board has to be recycled! Fresh water is sometimes sent there, but this is very expensive to do, so every drop of waste water is recycled.

This waste water includes sweat, water from the crew's breath, and even their urine is cleaned and recycled! The water goes through a VERY thorough cleaning process before it is consumed! This next activity explores how dirty water can be cleaned by filtering it through layers of materials.

YOU WILL NEED:

- a clean, empty 500 ml water bottle with a screw top lid
- scissors
- two cotton wool balls
- some sand
- some small gravel
- some large gravel
- some soil
- some water
- two small plastic cups

2

Tightly screw the lid in place. Push two cotton wool balls down into the bottle so they are packed tightly against the lid.

3

Add about 5 cm of sand on top of the cotton wool and about 5 cm of small gravel on top of the sand.

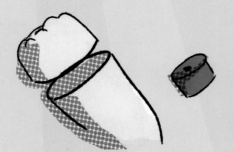

1

Cut the bottom off the drinks bottle. Ask an adult to help you make a small hole in the lid for the water to drip through.

4 Next put 5 cm of the large gravel on top of the small gravel. You now have four layers of filters in your bottle. Stand the whole thing upside down inside one of the cups (so the neck end is inside the cup).

5 Mix some water with the soil in the other cup to make muddy water. Pour it carefully into the bottle. The filters trap particles of dirt and the water in the cup should come out 'clean'.

Notice how each filter layer is made of a material that is bigger than the one below it. The top layer traps the biggest particles, the next layer traps smaller particles and the final layer – the cotton wool – traps the smallest particles.

DRINK ME?

The water is NOT yet clean enough to drink. If you want to drink the water you will have to boil it first (and let it cool down) to get rid of any bacteria.

SPACE FACT

One astronaut living on board the ISS for one year will use about 4,535 litres of water. To send that up into space would cost about £13 million!

23

MAKE YOUR OWN BLOOD!

The human body is simply not designed to survive in space. If you found yourself floating in space with no spacesuit on, the first thing that would happen is that the low-pressure vacuum of space would cause oxygen to escape out of your blood. Nitrogen in the blood near to your skin would collect in bubbles and your body would swell to twice its normal size!

Astronauts have to perform scientific experiments in space, often while wearing cumbersome gloves and other protective clothing. In this activity you will simulate working in a spacesuit as you create a model of human blood.

YOU WILL NEED:

- one small, clean, empty plastic box
- a bag of small, round, red sweets
- golden syrup
- some small marshmallows
- red cake sprinkles
- a spoon
- a pair of thin gloves
- a pair of thick gloves
- a pair of gardening gloves

1 Take everything outside as this could get messy. Put on the three pairs of gloves – the thinnest first and the gardening gloves last.

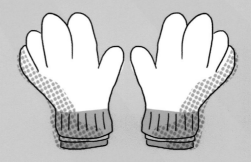

2 Half fill the plastic box with the golden syrup. This represents blood plasma, which is a thick liquid made almost entirely of water. Plasma makes up 55 per cent of human blood.

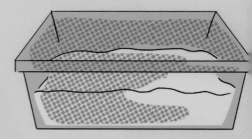

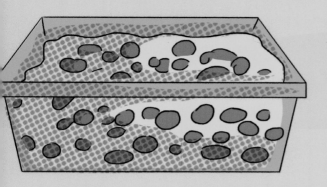

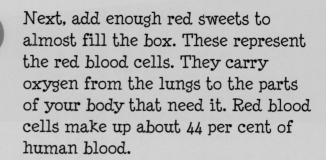

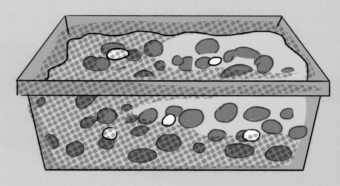

3 Next, add enough red sweets to almost fill the box. These represent the red blood cells. They carry oxygen from the lungs to the parts of your body that need it. Red blood cells make up about 44 per cent of human blood.

4 The marshmallows represent white blood cells. They protect the body from infection. They make up only 0.5 per cent of your blood, so only put a few in the box.

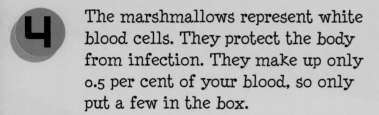

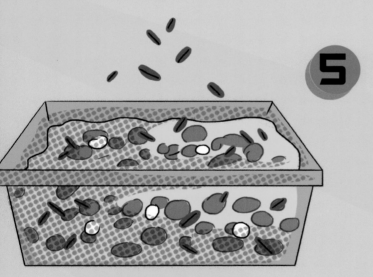

5 Finally, add some red cake sprinkles to represent platelets. They help to repair your body if you get a cut or graze. They make up 0.5 per cent of human blood, so add just a few sprinkles. Stir your mixture up.

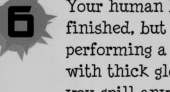

6 Your human blood model is finished, but how hard was performing a delicate task with thick gloves on? Did you spill any of the items? Think about how difficult it would be to perform tasks like this in space!

SPACE FACT

On Earth, gravity means that we have more blood in our lower bodies than our upper bodies. In space, the effect of fluid shift (see pages 10-11) spreads our blood out more evenly through the body. It also means our heads swell a little and our legs get a bit more skinny!

CREATE FLOATING BLOBS OF WATER

Turn on a tap and water will fall out. Water in a glass will stay at the bottom of the glass unless you knock it over, but even then it will fall to the floor. This is because Earth's force of gravity constantly pulls the water towards the ground.

In the weightlessness of space, objects seem to float. We call this free-fall because they are not actually floating. Water on a spacecraft is falling at the exact same speed as the spacecraft itself, so the water floats around in blobs rather than falling to the floor. This makes drinking or showering tricky! Few people will experience water blobs floating around in space, but you can replicate what it looks like in this activity, using vegetable oil and water.

YOU WILL NEED:

- a tall glass
- vegetable oil
- water
- food colouring (not yellow)
- a spoon

1 Half fill the tall glass with vegetable oil.

2 Fill the rest of the glass with water. Watch what happens.

3 Vegetable oil is less dense than water, so you will see the two liquids move around as they start to separate. The water will sink to the bottom of the glass and the vegetable oil will float on top of the water.

4 Carefully add a drop of food colouring to the oil and watch what happens. It should slowly sink to the bottom of the glass and mix with the water. It doesn't mix with the oil because it has a higher density than the oil.

5 Give the water and oil a stir with the spoon. You should see loads of little blobs of coloured water float around in the oil. This is exactly how water blobs move around in space.

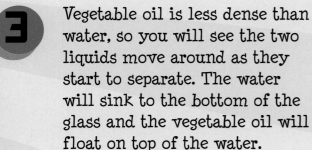

SCIENCE FACT

All liquids are made up of microscopic balls, called molecules. If you were to measure out exactly the same amount of oil and water, there would be fewer molecules in the oil than in the water. This is because oil is less dense than water.

COOK TOAST IN A SOLAR OVEN

Have you ever noticed that some spacecraft have shiny, golden panels sticking out of them? These are solar panels. They collect light energy from the Sun and turn it into electricity to power the spacecraft.

We can also use the heat, or infrared energy, from the Sun. If you ever get stuck on an alien planet, you might need a way to cook food. A great way to do this is to make a solar oven. It collects heat from the Sun and magnifies it to a temperature high enough to cook food. In this experiment you will make toast in your own solar oven!

YOU WILL NEED:

- an empty shoebox
- a pencil
- scissors
- aluminium foil
- PVA glue
- some black card
- cling film
- sticky tape
- two straws
- a small plate (small enough to fit inside the shoebox)
- a slice of bread

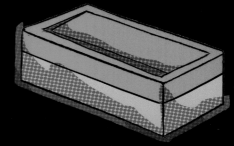

1 Draw a rectangle in the middle of the shoebox lid with a 3 cm border all the way around. Cut along two short and one long side of the rectangle to make a flap.

2 Glue the aluminium foil to the inside of the shoebox, including the lid and flap, with the shiniest side facing you.

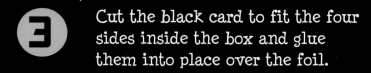

3 Cut the black card to fit the four sides inside the box and glue them into place over the foil.

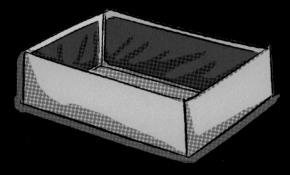

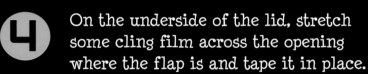

4 On the underside of the lid, stretch some cling film across the opening where the flap is and tape it in place.

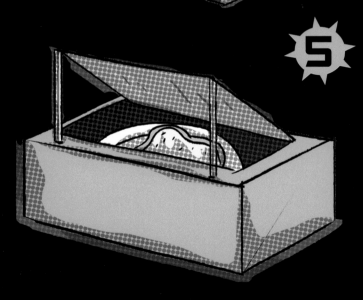

5 Now the good bit! Place the slice of bread on the plate and inside the box. Replace the lid. Put it in direct sunlight and prop the flap open with the straws. Check the bread regularly and before long you should have a piece of toast!

The foil concentrates the Sun's heat energy inside the box. The black card absorbs the heat (lighter colours would reflect back some of the heat), making the oven nice and toasty!

SPACE FACT

When an astronaut goes out on a spacewalk in direct sunlight, there is a danger that their spacesuit could act like a solar oven! Special materials help to keep out a lot of heat, but the astronaut will still get hot. To keep cool, they wear underwear that has lots of tubes inside it. Cold water runs through the tubes to keep the astronaut's body cool.

GLOSSARY

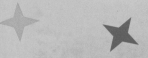

BACTERIA a microorganism that can often causes diseases

DENSITY the amount of material in a given area or space

ELECTRICITY a type of energy that can build up in one place and flow from one place to another

FILTER a device that removes solid items out of a liquid or a gas

FUNGUS an organism, such as a mushroom, that makes spores to reproduce and feeds on organic materials

GAS one of the three main states of matter. A gas can expand, squeeze, and flow from one place to another.

GRAVITY a force that tries to pull two objects together

HOSTILE unfriendly; a harsh environment

INSULATION a material that can be used to stop heat from escaping

ISS the International Space Station that orbits Earth

MAGNET an object that attracts most types of metal

MICROBE tiny organisms that can only be seen under a very powerful microscope

MICROMETEOROID the smallest pieces of space rock and dust; they usually weigh less than one gram

MICROWAVE a type of radiation with a wavelength longer than infrared, but shorter than radio waves

MOLECULES the building blocks of all matter. Each molecule is made of a group of atoms.

NITROGEN a gas with no smell or colour. It is a chemical element usually represented by the letter N.

ORBIT a circular or oval path one object follows around another

ORGANISM a living things, such as a plant or an animal

OXYGEN a gas with no smell or colour that is essential for life on Earth. It is a chemical element usually represented by the letter O.

PARTICLE a tiny object that makes up matter. Atoms are the smallest particles.

RADIATION one of the ways that energy travels through space

SOLAR relating to the Sun

TARDIGRADE a small but very tough, eight-legged creature that lives in water; also called a water bear

TRANSPARENT a material that allows light to pass through it

URINE a watery, usually yellow liquid that transports waste out of the body

WEIGHTLESSNESS the effect felt by astronauts when they are in orbit around Earth, which lets them float around

YEAST a microscopic fungus made of cells that can reproduce, and change sugar into alcohol and carbon dioxide

FURTHER INFORMATION

BOOKS

Adventures in STEAM: Space by Richard Spilsbury (Wayland, 2017)
Astronaut Academy by Steve Martin & Jennifer Farley (Ivy Press, 2016)
The International Space Station by Clive Gifford (Wayland, 2018)
Living in Space by Katie Daynes (Usborne, 2006)
Research on the Edge: Space by Angela Royston (Wayland, 2015)

PLACES TO VISIT

National Space Centre, Leicester
Science Museum, London
Life Science Centre, Newcastle
Glasgow Science Centre, Glasgow

WEBSITES

A section of the NASA website that explains what it is like to live on the International Space Station.
www.nasa.gov/audience/foreducators/stem-on-station/dayinthelife

BBC Bitesize is a great website with lots of curriculum-based science activities.
www.bbc.com/education

The ESA Kids website has loads of information about living in space.
www.esa.int/esaKIDSen/LifeinSpace.html

INDEX

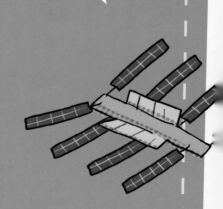

SPACE SCIENCE

TITLES IN THIS SERIES

Born in Norfolk, author **MARK THOMPSON** has had a fascination with all things in the sky ever since he was a small boy. At the age of 10 he got his first view through a telescope; Saturn in all its glory. It ignited a passion that has stayed with him ever since.

Mark has inspired millions of viewers to get out and enjoy the night sky through his role as presenter on the RTS nominated show *BBC Stargazing Live*. His passion for reaching out to a new audience has found him working on *The One Show*, *This Morning*, Channel 4 documentaries and ITV's prime time breakfast show, *Good Morning*. He is also a regular face on *BBC Breakfast*, *Five News* and a regular voice on *Radio Five Live*.

SCIENCE FOR EXPLORING OUTER SPACE

Out of This World
Hunt for Meteorites
Erupt a Martian Volcano!
Smash into the Moon
'Talk' Like a Computer
Freeze a Comet
Create Gravity ... in a Bucket!

Bend Water ... with a Comb
Explore Venus's Atmosphere
Make a Fruit Solar System
Whip Up a Storm ... in a Bottle
Find the Speed of Light ... with Cheese!
Supercool Water

SCIENCE FOR LOOKING INTO SPACE

Staring into Space
Measure the Moon
See Where the Sun ... Sets
Observe Earth's Spin
Tell the Time ... with Shadows
Build a Telescope
Observe the Sun

Become the Lunar Phases
Hunt for Alien Worlds
Create Colours ... with a Spectroscope
Explore the Doppler Effect
Capture Star Trails
Build an Astrolobe

SCIENCE FOR ROCKETING INTO SPACE

Reach for the Stars
Escape Gravity
Overcome Inertia ... with an egg
Explore Epic Exothermic Eruptions
Balloon to the Moon
Lower the Centre of Gravity
Blast Off ... with a Chemical Reaction

Launch a Straw Rocket ... with Puff Power
Hurtle to Earth on an 'Eggciting' Mission
Send a Rocket into Orbit
Make Water Weightless
Become a Rocket Booster
Launch the Ultimate Rocket!

SCIENCE FOR SURVIVING IN SPACE

A Dangerous Place
Pack a Space Bag
Inflate a Balloon ... with Microbes
Eat Like an Astronaut
Warm Up with Insulation
Shield Yourself from Meteoroids
Grow Food in Space

Draw a Magnetic Force Field
Make a Biosphere ... in a Jar!
Make Dirty Water Clean (ish!)
Make Your Own Blood
Create Floating Blobs of Water
Cook Toast in a Solar Oven

www.markthompsonastronomy.com   www.spectacularscienceshow.com